TAKING THE STEAM OUT OF WALLPAPER REMOVAL

VIRGINIA M. YOST

ROGUE WAVE PUBLISHING
P.O. BOX 7921   BERKELEY, CA 94707

531 9561

TAKING THE STEAM OUT OF WALLPAPER REMOVAL.

Library of Congress Cataloging-in-Publication Data

Yost, Virginia M., 1940–
    Taking the steam out of wallpaper removal.

    1. Paper-hanging. 2. Wallpaper. I. Title.
TH8441.Y58 1986   698'.6   86–10088
ISBN 0-938005-04-9

CONTENTS

INTRODUCTION

Removing wallpaper is not difficult and this book is an honest attempt to demystify the process. By taking you through an easy to follow, step-by-step procedure, we hope to put this dreaded project into perspective.

Papering or painting over old wallcovering is always risky. The moisture in the paint or the wallpaper adhesive will serve to loosen the old wallcovering and this could cost you much more in time and money than facing up to the removal project in the first place. Taking the old covering off is your best bet.

The information contained in this book will let you achieve expert results as well as save a substantial amount of money; which you will surely be able to use toward the more fun parts of your decorating project.

Anyone who has ever faced a wallpaper steamer will be relieved and amazed after using the methods described in this book. You will have better results without the hassle and danger associated with using a rented steamer.

Now that you have the information to take the hard part out of your redecorating project, you can relax and enjoy it.

THE THREE WAYS TO REMOVE WALLCOVERINGS

Regardless of what your redecorating plans may be, once you have decided to get down to the bare walls before you begin, you will be glad to know that there are only three basic ways to remove wallpaper.

The first, and by far the easiest method, is by stripping it off the walls dry. Many modern wallcoverings are manufactured so that they may removed for easy redecoration simply by pulling them off the walls. This is done without wetting the walls with water or chemicals and is therefore a fairly tidy operation.

Some very old paper-based wallcoverings can also be removed dry. When the adhesive has deteriorated, the paper can be scraped off. It is not practical however, to get all of the old wallpaper off in an entire room this way.

Steaming is the second method we will be examining here. Sometimes referred to as "the dreaded way", and rightly so, it is surprisingly the most common method used by the do-it-yourselfer. This, despite the fact that it is the most expensive as well as the most dangerous method.

The steamer looks like a very large bread box which is filled with hot water, plugged into a wall socket and allowed to heat and make steam. A metal paddle, attached to the box with a long rubber hose, is held up to the wall. The steam escapes through small holes in the paddle and penetrates the paper to soften the adhesive. The paddle is then removed to an adjacent area while the loosened covering is scraped off the wall.

It is at this point that your problems begin. You are now trying to do two things at once: steaming and scraping. After a short time your arms will start to ache and you will want to put the paddle down, but they didn't tell you that there is no shut-off valve on it. It just keeps pouring out the steam until you unplug the steamer and the water cools off enough to stop sending the steam through the hose and out the little holes in the paddle.

In addition, you now have wet wallpaper and gooey old paste all over your other hand and arm; not to mention your shoes, to which all of it is sticking as you walk along next to the wall. And when you've just about reached the end of your rope, you come to the end of your hose. It should be noted here that moving the steamer takes a little muscle when it is empty; once full of boiling water, this apparatus is not any easier to move.

While steam itself is an effective tool in the removal of wallcovering because it can penetrate deeply, the use of the rented wallpaper steamer has many drawbacks; not the least of these being the danger factor. Extreme care must be taken with the steam to avoid burns. It has also been our experience that very hot water comes out of the paddle in addition to the steam.

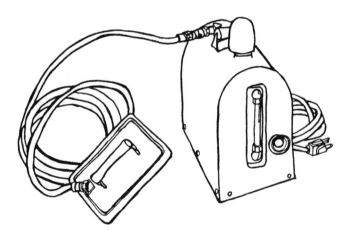

The steaming method is also very slow since you can only remove a 1' x 2' area at a time. It is hot, sticky and wet. Protection of furniture and floors is absolutely necessary.

And the bottom line . . . you've just spent the better part of the day steaming and scraping old wallpaper off your bedroom walls, you're hot and tired and need to relax. Before you will be finished for the day, you have to unplug the steamer, let the water cool, clean up the paddle, empty out the left over water, load the stuff in the car and get it down to the equipment rental shop before they close at 5:30 pm. Plus, you have to pay $20.00!

Now you say, "There must be an easier way!" There is. The spray method.

The spray method, that is wetting, soaking and scraping, is not, contrary to popular belief, a new method. The old-timers used hot water mixed with vinegar and applied it to the walls with a sponge. Progress has given us a liquid chemical and the garden sprayer.

This method requires preparing the surface of the wallcovering for penetration by a chemical wallpaper remover or wetting agent, mixed with water, which will be sprayed on the wall. This preparation can be done with a variety of aids, ranging from coarse sandpaper or wire brush to an old saw or a scarfrier. Which tool you use will depend on the type of wallcovering with which you are dealing.

Once you apply this liquid to the walls with an ordinary garden sprayer, you will need the patience to let it soak in and do its job. Usually within 30 minutes, the softened wallcovering is ready to be easily removed with a broadknife.

Many years of experience have proven that the spray

method of wetting, soaking and scraping, is the clear choice for both the do-it-yourselfer and the professional alike. Excellent results can be obtained quickly and efficiently with a minimum of fuss and expense.

Liquid wallpaper removers are available at most paint and wallpaper stores for less than $5.00. Garden sprayers cost under $25.00 while wallpaper steamers go for around $400.00.

We will be detailing the spray method throughout this book. If you follow the step-by-step instructions, you will achieve professional results as well as the satisfaction of doing a job in the least painful way possible.

Any job is easier

when you have

the right tools . . .

TOOLS

- a) wide putty knife (4" broadknife)
- b) regular putty knife (1½"-2" stiff)
- c) screw driver
- d) wallpaper shaver
- e) garden sprayer (2-3 gallons)
- f) single edge razor blade

OPTIONAL TOOLS

- g) scarifier
- h) wire brush
- i) hand saw
- j) power sander

SUPPLIES

- k) wallpaper removing chemical
- l) disposable plastic drop cloths
- m) large plastic garbage bag(s)
- n) masking tape (1"-1½")
- o) hot water
- p) large sponge and medium size bucket
- q) sandpaper (50 and 80 grit) and a sanding block

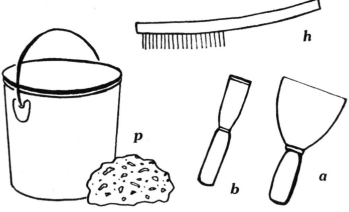

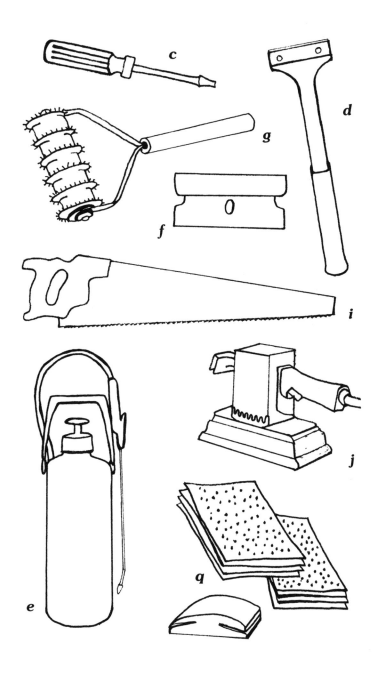

c

d

g

f

i

e

j

q

9

TESTING TO SEE
WHAT YOU'VE GOT

THE WALLS

It is necessary to know whether you have drywall or lath and plaster walls when you are removing wallcovering. Once you have determined the type of walls you will be working with, you can make the best use of the tools available and get the job done with a maximum of ease.

Drywall is the material generally used in houses built after the early 1940's. It is a sheet of chalk-like substance, 5/8" thick, covered with a facing of lightweight cardboard. These carboard-faced sheets are nailed over wood-framed walls and are hollow sounding when rapped on with your knuckles.

Lath and plaster construction was nearly always used prior to the early 1940's. It consists of 1½" wide wood lath nailed to wood-framed walls and then covered with two or three coats of plaster. These walls are more solid and sound duller when rapped on.

For wallcovering removal purposes, drywall is a little more delicate, requiring more care when scrapping to avoid damaging the cardboard facing. Lath and plaster walls can take more energetic scraping with the sharper wallpaper shaving tool.

If you have any doubts about the kind of walls you are working with, consult someone you trust. It is important to have this information.

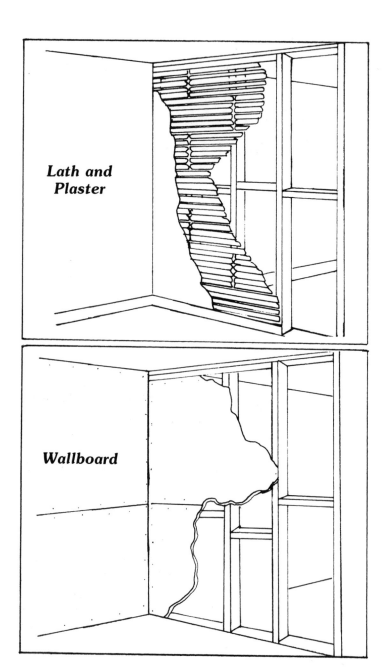

Lath and Plaster

Wallboard

THE PAPER

The next step is to determine what kind of wallcovering you will be removing so you can use the appropriate method. Here's what to do.

1. Take a putty knife, and in a corner or seam at the bottom of the wall, pry up the edge and try to pull the wallcovering up. If it comes away from the wall and keeps coming as you pull, then it is strippable; the easiest type to remove.

2. If, instead, the paper immediately starts to tear as you pull up, it is non-strippable. You will now need to determine which type of wallpaper it is.

Check the following list to make this determination and then refer to the appropriate section for methods of removal.

VARIOUS TYPES
OF WALLCOVERING

Strippable Wallcoverings are those which can be completely removed from the wall without scraping or using liquid remover.

Peelable Wallcoverings are those with a top layer (usually vinyl) which strips off without scraping or using liquid remover; leaving a layer of paper backing on the wall. You will need to remove this with the liquid remover.

Paper Wallcoverings, otherwise known as "regular old wallpaper," is a paper-based wallcovering that has no vinyl coating. You will know this is what you have when a spongeful of water is held up to its surface and it readily soaks in and spreads.

Vinyl Wallcoverings are made from a liquid or flexible film, heat-bonded to a fabric or paper backing. Vinyls are truly the most durable wallcoverings because of their scrubability and imperviousness to moisture.

Vinyl Coated Wallcoverings have a thin coating of vinyl applied over regular paper, making it less porous. In the lower price range, this is one of the most common types of wallcoverings produced today.

Foils and Mylars are wallcoverings made of very thin, flexible metallic sheets of either aluminum or simulated metal, laminated to a paper or fabric backing. Some are mylar coated for a very reflective finish.

Flocked Wallcoverings are made by printing a design on paper with a slow drying paint/ink and sifting nylon or rayon fabric fibers over it, resulting in a two-dimensional effect. Flocks are often peelable.

Grass Cloth, Cork, and Burlap Wallcoverings are usually handmade of natural fibers glued to paper backing. Grass cloth wallcoverings are hand dyed and woven, resulting in color and texture variations within each roll. Corks are natural or simulated and pressed into thin sheets which are glued to paper backing. Burlaps have the look of rough fabric, are sometimes dyed, and are glued to a paper backing. These types of wallcoverings are rarely strippable and must be removed with a liquid remover.

Textile Wallcoverings are actual fabrics, glued or stapled to the wall. Felt is included in this category.

Photo Murals on the market today are made of several pieces and are mainly dry-strippable. The older type of mural, that looks more like a painting than a photograph, is usually a paper-based wallcovering.

Canvas Wallcoverings were often used over old plaster walls to conceal cracks and make the walls even for painting or other decorations. If you run into this canvas layer under wallcovering you are removing; LEAVE IT ON!

STEP-BY-STEP
INSTRUCTIONS

PREPARATION

Good preparation will make your job go smoother and is worth a little extra time at the beginning. You can then give your full attention to your project without a lot of stopping and starting.

1) Take everything off the walls, put away all the knick knacks, and remove as much furniture as possible from the area where you'll be working. Leave the switch plates and plug covers in place for now. They will keep the water away from the electrical wires.

2) On the floor along the base of the wall(s) you'll be working on, place some old towels or bedspreads that you don't mind getting wet. Then spread out the plastic drops over the towels and tape them to the baseboards in several places. This will keep the water from running onto the floors. It is also a good idea to hang plastic drops over doorways while spray is being used.

3) Cover any furniture left in the room to protect it from overspray.

4) Bring all the tools you might need into the room so you won't have to make another trip out to the work bench in the garage. Check the tool and supply list on page 8.

5) Give yourself a full day for an average size room and an easy removal. Allow two days for a a problem situation or a many layered removal.

6) Now you are ready to get into the project. Look to the section which applies to the wallcovering you have determined you have for step-by-step removal instructions.

Good Luck!

REMOVAL OF
STRIPPABLE WALLCOVERINGS

You will know from your test piece, or if you put the wallcovering up yourself, if you have strippable paper. To remove it, just grasp a lower corner and pull the covering away from the wall until you have both lower corners free. Then take hold of the bottom edge with both hands and pull until the entire strip is off the wall. Repeat this procedure with each strip around the room.

When you have finished, turn to page 37, *After It's Off,* for information on preparing the walls for painting or repapering.

Removing strippable wallcoverings is very satisfying and gives a powerful feeling as you are ripping it off the wall. It is also very fast, so make sure you've removed all the pictures and knick-knacks from the walls before you get caught up in the fun.

Fabric-backed Vinyls are usually strippable wallcoverings. They are found mainly in bathrooms and kitchens because they are so resistant to moisture.

Occasionally, fabric-backed vinyls will present a problem in removal if they have been applied to drywall which has had only a thin coat of paint or no sealer at all.

When you pull on the wallcovering, if the facing paper layer of the drywall comes away with it, STOP! Try to separate the vinyl front from the fabric backing. If you get the vinyl off separately, you can spray the fabric that is left on the walls with the liquid remover and then pull or scrape it off in strips.

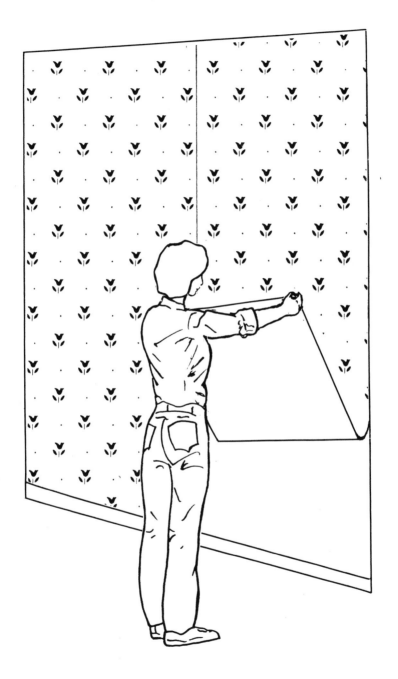

If the vinyl will not separate from the fabric backing, you must then choose whether to remove the wallcovering and repair the drywall damage or to leave well enough alone. See section on *Unsealed Wallboard*, page 34.

The final step is to turn to page 37. *After It's Off*, for information on how to prepare the walls for painting or new wallcovering.

REMOVAL OF
PEELABLE WALLCOVERINGS

With peelable wallcoverings, the vinyl or facing part comes off like strippable wallcoverings. Just grasp a lower corner and pull the covering away from the wall until you have both lower corners free. Then take hold of the bottom edge with both hands and pull until the entire strip is off the wall. The paper or fabric backing will stay on the wall.

After you have all the vinyl peeled off the walls, fill the garden sprayer with hot water and liquid wallpaper remover, and follow the instructions listed in the next section to remove the backing material from the wall.

REMOVAL OF
PAPER WALLCOVERINGS

1) Follow preparation steps listed on page 19.

2) For a whole room, fill the garden sprayer with hot water and add the removal chemical according to the manufacturer's instructions. If you are only doing one wall, reduce the quantity accordingly.

3) Spray the first wall *thoroughly* with the nozzle open to a wide mist. Adjust the nozzle to the thin single line spray for use near the unpapered walls or ceilings. After spraying the second wall, wait 10-30 minutes for the chemicals to soften the adhesive on the back of the paper.

While you are waiting, mop up any water that collects at the base of the walls with the sponge, squeezing it into a bucket you can keep handy.

4) Go back to the first wall you sprayed and you should be able to see the paper *bubbling up*. This means it is ready to be scrapped off with a broadknife.

If it is not bubbling up or looks like it is drying out, spray the entire wall again thoroughly. Usually several sprayings are necessary before the paper will release easily from the wall.

If you have kept the paper wet and it has soaked long enough, it will be easy to remove. The paper gets about as soft as wet newspaper. A good comparison is to think of how long it takes to soak a label off a jar. If you start scraping too soon you wind up hacking away at it. If it soaks long enough, it releases with ease . . . well, easier.

Be patient.

5) Repeat the process of spraying the next two walls, letting it soak and then scraping to finish off the room.

6) Remove the switch plates and plug covers and carefully finish up around them.

7) The final step is to turn to page 37, *After It's Off,* for information on how to prepare the walls for painting or new wallcovering.

While a garden sprayer is the easiest and most efficient tool to use for controlling the water mess, if you can't buy, borrow or rent one, there are a few alternatives.

The wallpaper remover/hot water mixture may be applied from a bucket with large sponge or your regular kitchen sponge mop. A fluffy long napped paint roller will hold a lot of liquid and spread it on the walls. Even an ordinary plastic sprayer bottle used for household cleaners or plant misting will do the job in a pinch.

The idea is to get the solution on the walls and keep them wet long enough to loosen the wallcoverings. We use the garden sprayer because it is the quickest and neatest way to wet the largest area.

REMOVAL OF
NON-STRIPPABLE VINYL
COATED WALLCOVERINGS

1) Follow preparation steps listed on page 19.
2) Break the surface of the vinyl with coarse sand-paper (50 or 60 grit) on a sanding block or power sander. The coating is fairly thin, so a light sanding is enough.

If the removal of this type of wallcovering is extensive, i.e., several rooms, or there are many layers on the walls, you might want to buy a scarifier. It is a tool which has several rows of teeth on a roller. Some are available with the teeth on a sponge roller. This tool costs around $10.00.

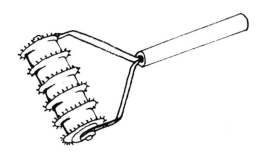

When the scarifier is rolled over the surface of the walls, the teeth puncture the vinyl coating on the wallcovering allowing the liquid wallpaper remover to penetrate.

The vinyl surface may also be broken with a wire brush by scraping it over the wallcovering hard enough to scratch through the vinyl coating.

An old saw blade may be used to break the surface by drawing the whole cutting edge against the walls in all directions.

3) The next step is to spray the walls with the liquid wallpaper remover and scrape the paper off. Follow the step-by-step instructions beginning on page 23, in the section on *Removal of Paper Wallcoverings*.

4) The final step is to turn to page 37, *After It's Off*, to prepare the walls for painting or new wallcovering.

REMOVAL OF
FOILS, MYLARS AND
FLOCKED WALLCOVERINGS

These wallcoverings fall into one of the removal categories covered on previous pages. They will be strippable, peelable or non-strippable, so once you test and determine which type you are dealing with you can follow the instructions in the appropriate section.

If you determine that you will be removing non-strippable foil or mylar wallcovering, you will find that sandpaper does not work very well for breaking the surface to allow penetration by the liquid remover.

In this case it is better to use the wallpaper shaver to make many slices in the wallcovering. Be sure to hold the tool at a 45 degree angle to the wall for the best results. You may also use a scarifier, as described on page 26.

REMOVAL OF
GRASSCLOTH AND CORK
WALLCOVERINGS

These removals are pretty wet because the fibers absorb so much water, but are also easy. The fibers are glued to a paper backing so this is a two step removal process.

First the front fibers, the grass part, will loosen and bubble up. These will scrape off in long strips like wet fabric.

After all the facing is off, you will have to re-wet the paper backing that is left on the walls. Wait for it to bubble up, re-wetting areas that dryout, and then scrape the paper off.

Removing cork is exactly the same process as grasscloth except that the front fibers are cork and come off in small chunks instead of big strips. The cork absorbs a lot of moisture, so keep it wet.

1) Follow the preparation steps listed on page 19.

2) Follow the step-by-step instructions beginning on page 23, *Removal of Paper Wallcoverings.*

3) The final step is to turn to page 37, *After It's Off,* for information on how to prepare the walls for painting or new wallcovering.

OTHER SITUATIONS . . .

Common and Not

PAINTED OVER
WALLCOVERINGS

In order to remove wallpaper that is under one or more layers of paint, the painted surface must be broken to allow the liquid remover to penetrate and soften the adhesive. This is done in one of the following ways:

1) Coarse sandpaper on a sanding block or on a power sander will efficiently break the surface when you are dealing with a relatively small area.

2) A scarifier rolled over the surface firmly enough to break into the paint, but not hard enough to damage the walls is a good method for walls with many layers of paint over the paper. See illustration on page 26.

3) The shaving tool held at a 45 degree angle is effective in making many slices for the liquid to get through. See illustration on page 28.

After the surface is broken, follow the steps on page 23. Removing painted over wallcovering is slow because of slow penetration of the liquid remover so be sure to really break the surface and saturate it well.

MANY LAYERS OF PAPER

When removing many layers of paper, start by following the step-by-step instructions on page 23. It is important to keep the walls as wet as possible to facilitate penetration by the liquid remover.

Sometimes the layers come off virtually one at a time, with constant rewetting necessary. If you are trying to remove three or four layers, use the scarifier or shaving tool to break through the layers and hasten chemical penetration. See the scarifier illustration on page 26 and the shaving tool illustration on page 28. With good penetration by the chemical you may find that several layers come off at once.

You may run into a layer, after one or two are off, which was sealed with paint. Since everything is wet, you cannot very well use sandpaper to break that surface, so use the shaver tool, your saw blade or scarifier instead.

Some say a church key type can opener will work for breaking the surface when you run into a painted over layer. It will work all right in a pinch, but it is hard enough to control how deep you are scrapping and you will probably spend a lot of time filing in the many gouges in the wall.

UNSEALED WALLBOARD . . .

Or when to leave well enough alone.

Once in a while, usually in new construction, drywall will not be sealed with a thick enough coat of paint to allow removal of wallcovering without *extensive* damage to the walls.

The situation becomes clear during testing, when the gray cardboard-like facing of the wallboard tears off with the wallcovering; or when, after wetting, the wallcovering simply won't come off without tearing the wallboard.

When the test area proves this to be the case, LEAVE THE WALLCOVERING ON THE WALL!

Glue down any loose pieces and fill in any uneven areas and seams which may have separated or are overlapped. Then seal the whole wall with oil-based enamel undercoat or a good primer/sealer. A special type sealer is required over heavy vinyls so check with your paint dealer.

If the seams in an entire room are separated or overlapped, you may wish to use joint compound instead of spackle to fill in and smooth over the rough spots. See the instructions for this procedure on page 40.

A CANVAS LAYER

If in your removal project you get the layers of wallcovering off and find a canvas covering on the original plaster walls, *leave it on.* This treatment was used on lath and plaster walls and ceilings when they were to be painted. It helped preserve the plaster, kept cracks from showing and got the walls nice and smooth.

If the canvas is loose in a few places, glue it back down. If it is in such bad shape that you cannot glue it or patch it with spackle or joint compound, you will be forced to remove it.

When you take off this canvas layer, be prepared for most of the finish coat of plaster to come with it and to have to resurface those walls. Usually the canvas is so heavily painted, pulling it off dry is the only way to get it off; leaving you with walls which need lots of patching. If you can scarify and wet it, the removal will probably leave the walls in a little better condition.

Turn to page 37, *After It's Off,* for information on how to repair the walls.

AFTER IT'S OFF

AFTER IT'S OFF

So, now it's off. You are standing there surveying your handiwork with a happy smile on your face. Take a few minutes to pat yourself on the back. You deserve it!

Once the wallcovering is off, you are ready to really begin your redecorating project. Good wall preparation is the cornerstone of a lasting, quality job that you will be proud of. Now is the time to fill all holes and do any other wall repair.

This section will outline the uses of various materials used for repairing damaged walls, how to remove mildew and kill the spores, as well as how to get the walls ready for painting or repapering.

WALL PREP MATERIALS

The three basic patching materials we work with are *Fix-All* or *Quik-Fix* (both brand names), spackle and joint compound.

Fix-All and *Quik-Fix* are both fast-setting interior patching compounds used to repair cracks and holes in plaster, wallboard and wood surfaces. These products are best used for gouges or holes deeper than 1/2" and wider than 2 or 3 inches. Both products are non-shrinking and, in fact, expand a little when they dry.

Because they dry very hard, they are difficult to sand, so be sure to allow a little room for this slight swelling.

You will want to fill a deep hole mostly with Fix-All and then finish it off with joint compound or spackle.

Spackling compound is the material used to fill all the small holes left from the pictures and knick-knacks you removed from the walls. It is also used for small cracks and gouges. Spackle dries fairly fast and is best used for small areas. Application with a flexible putty knife should be as smooth as possible to avoid excessive sanding after it dries.

Joint compound is the material we use when resurfacing an entire wall or when preparing to paper over old wallcovering and need to smooth out the seams. We also use it to smooth out the texture on a wall or a textured wallcovering that cannot be removed. More than one coat is usually required to fill in a textured surface because joint compound shrinks as it dries.

Having the consistency of peanut butter, joint compound is applied with a broadknife and is very slow drying. It is this slow drying quality that makes it easy to work with. The edges of patched areas can be easily sanded when dry. They may also be smoothed out with a wet sponge when almost dry; eliminating the mess from sanding dust. The smoother you apply it to the wall in the first place, the less sanding or smoothing you'll have to do later.

REPAIRING
DAMAGED DRYWALL

If pieces of the paper facing came loose during removal of the wallcoverings, repair it now.

Let the damaged areas dry thoroughly and cut away any tails of paper with a razor blade.

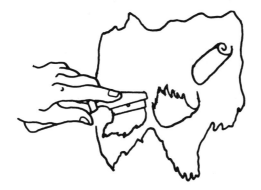

Carefully trim away tears in drywall with a single edge razor blade.

Seal the area with a spray sealer such as *Kilz* or *Stain Lock Sealer.* Let that dry and then fill any depressions with spackle to blend with the surface of the wall. After the spackle dries hard, sand it lightly, and continue your wall preparation for painting or repapering.

Use your broadknife to spread spackling compound over damaged areas.

PREPARING WALLS
FOR PAINTING

Be sure all the old adhesive is completely removed from the walls. Adhesive is a poor base over which to apply apint.

To illustrate this important point, let us tell you about one situation we encountered.

Grasscloth had been steamed off in an office leaving a thick coat of sticky adhesive. The walls were then painted with a flat wall paint. When some cracks appeared in the paint, a second coat was applied. Again, as the paint started to dry, a myriad of cracks appeared. it was at this point that we got a call for help.

The adhesive which had been softened with the steam, and then again with the paint, was drying slower than the latex paint thus causing the cracks in the paint as it dried. We wet the walls with warm water and then scraped both the paint and the adhesive off with broadknives. We then sponged off the last remaining sticky film. When the walls dried, another coat of paint was applied.

The moral of the story: **Clean the old adhesive off those walls before you paint them!**

To remove adhesive, wet all walls with warm water, using either the garden sprayer or a sponge. While they are wet, scrape off the adhesive with the broadknife. You can use a small bucket edge for wiping the adhesive from your knife. The last step is to wash the walls with warm water to remove the final film of adhesive.

*Be sure to sponge off that final sticky film before ap-
plying any paint to the wall.*

PREPARING WALLS
FOR NEW WALLCOVERING

Even though wallcovering conceals many imperfec-
tions, a smooth surface is a must in order to insure satisfying final results.

Leave the old adhesive on the walls to act as a siz-
ing for the new wallcovering. If it is very rough, sand
it lightly with 80 grit sandpaper, and brush the dust off.

If there are real crators in the old adhesive, and you
are going to install an exceptionally smooth covering
like a foil, mylar or one with a white or shiny
background, then remove the old adhesive.

Wet the old adhesive with warm water and scrape
it off, or those peaks and valleys will show right through
the slick new wallcovering. This procedure is fully

described in the previous section on preparing to paint. Once you have removed the old adhesive, check the walls for any nicks or gouges that might also show through the new paper and be sure to fill those in and seal them at this time.

REMOVAL OF MILDEW

The growth of fungus that causes mildew is encouraged in damp, warm, unventilated areas like behind vinyl wallcoverings.

If mildew is growing on any areas, now is the time to remove it and to kill the spores so it will not grow back. This is done by scrubbing the walls with a sponge and a solution of the following:

1/3 cup TSP (trisodium phosphate)
2½ tablespoons heavy duty detergent
2 cups cholorine bleach
1½ quarts warm water

After scouring the walls, rinse with clean water. Let the walls dry overnight. Then roll on a coat of oil-based enamel undercoat to which mildew retardant has been added. This will seal the walls and keep the fungus growth down. After the undercoat has dried, the paper can then be hung.

ARE YOU

AN OLD

HOUSE LOVER?

ARE YOU AN OLD HOUSE LOVER?

If you are, and you own one, you may have a whole history of your house in the wallpaper you remove. You might want to start a house history scrapbook as you proceed through your renovation projects. If you already have one started, including samples of wallpaper you unearth can be a very interesting addition.

It is a good idea to take a color photograph, before any removal attempts are made, for your records. The graphic information will be preserved, in case the wallcovering cannot be removed in any salvagable way.

Scraps of wallpaper will often come off dry because old adhesives have completely deteriorated. So before you begin using a liquid remover, work a broadknife between the plaster wall and the first layer of wallpaper and carefully scrape. If you wind up with a chunk of wallpaper made up of many layers, or you cannot get your knife down to the plaster, you can use a steam iron to loosen the adhesive enough to separate the layers.

Lay the pieces on waxed paper or something they won't stick to until they are dry. Then the samples can be preserved between sheets of cardboard or mounted and displayed like art work.

Suggested places to find old wallpaper include under wood paneling, door jambs, molding or other woodwork which has been added on after original construction.

In the process of removing wallcovering, if you discover something you think might be historically valuable, usually pre-dating the nineteenth century, contact a museum. They can advise you on special removal, conservation and mounting. There are also commercial firms who do wallpaper removal for conservation purposes.

The Cooper-Hewitt Museum of Decorative Arts and Design has one of the most extensive collections of 18th and 19th century wallpaper in the United States.

If you have any questions about what you find in your home, send a sample along with information about the house, date of construction, and location the samples were found to:

> Ms. Ann Hysa Dorfsman
> Keeper of the Wallpaper Collection
> Cooper-Hewitt Museum
> 2 East, 91th Street
> New York, NY 10028

Virginia M. Yost

About the Author

The author has been self-employed for over 10 years and has specialized in the installation and removal of wallcoverings for the last seven years.

She is the mother of three children, a licensed cosmetologist, a former bookstore owner, a skilled seamstress and an avid do-it-yourselfer.

Born and raised in the San Francisco bay area, her father was a union master painter for 32 years.

Already a successful painter when she entered the paperhanging field, she discovered the lack of good written information on the subject; especially about removal of wallcoverings. There simply did not exist a comprehensive, step-by-step "how-to" book.

Based on the expertise gained from years of experience, she has written this book to fill that need for professionals and amateurs alike.

Send us your comments

Feedback on material contained in this book is invited. We are interested in knowing any special tricks you find that work well and any new tools you may have discovered or designed.

Also let us know if you have encountered any special problems that we did not discuss in this book.

Write to: Virginia M. Yost
c/o Rogue Wave Publishing
P.O. Box 7921
Berkeley, CA 94707.

ROGUE WAVE PUBLISHING
P.O. BOX 7921
BERKELEY, CA 94707-0921

TELEPHONE (415) 763-1264

PLEASE SEND ME _____ COPIES OF TAKING
THE STEAM OUT OF WALLPAPER REMOVAL.

ENCLOSED IS $4.95 EACH PLUS $1.00 FOR
SHIPPING AND HANDLING OF THE FIRST
BOOK AND 50¢ FOR EACH ADDITIONAL BOOK.

____ I CANNOT WAIT 3-4 WEEKS FOR BOOK
RATE. ENCLOSED IS AN ADDITIONAL $1
PER BOOK FOR AIR MAIL.

____ PLEASE ADD MY NAME TO YOUR MAILING
LIST FOR NOTIFICATION OF OTHER BOOKS
BY VIRGINIA M. YOST OR OTHER DO-IT-
YOURSELF PUBLICATIONS.

ORDER
BY
MAIL